CONTENTS

Who was Boudica? 4

Boudica's life story 6

Celtic Britain 8

Celtic beliefs 10

Clothes and hairstyles 12

The Romans arrive 14

The death of Prasutagus 16

Warrior queen 18

Boudica attacks Colchester 20

The uprising continues 22

How do we know? 24

What happened next? 26

Boudica lives on 28

Timeline 30

Glossary and quiz 31

Index and answers 32

WHO WAS BOUDICA?

Boudica led an uprising against the Romans, who had invaded Britain in CE 43. The aim of the uprising was to chase the Roman army from the shores of Britain.

This statue of Boudica stands near the Houses of Parliament in London.

Who was Boudica?

We do not know very much about Boudica. Most of what we do know was written by two Roman historians, writing after her death (see pages 24–25). They tell us that she came from an important family. She married King Prasutagus of the Iceni tribe and they had two daughters.

FASCINATING FACTS

BOUDICA CAN BE SPELT SEVERAL DIFFERENT WAYS: BOUDICA, BOUDICCA AND BOADICEA. HISTORIANS TODAY PREFER BOUDICA OR BOUDICCA. HER NAME IS LINKED TO THE CELTIC WORD FOR VICTORY.

King Prasutagus' head appears on this coin dating from CE 40–50.

BOUDICA
and the
CELTS

DAVID GILL

W
FRANKLIN WATTS
LONDON·SYDNEY

Franklin Watts

Published in Great Britain in paperback in 2018 by
The Watts Publishing Group

Copyright © The Watts Publishing Group 2016

Series editor: Julia Bird
Editor: Sarah Ridley
Series designer: Matt Lilly
Picture researcher: Diana Morris

ISBN 978 1 4451 6353 6

FSC
www.fsc.org
MIX
Paper from
responsible sources
FSC® C104740

Printed in China

Franklin Watts
An imprint of
Hachette Children's Group
Part of The Watts Publishing Group
Carmelite House
50 Victoria Embankment
London EC4Y 0DZ

An Hachette UK Company

www.hachette.co.uk
www.franklinwatts.co.uk

Picture credits: Antphotos/Dreamstime: 26. CFimages/Alamy: 23, 31.
Colchester Museum Services: 2b, 15t, 15c, 20. Jeff Dalton/Dreamstime:
10tl. Detail Heritage/Alamy: 17. Claudio Divizia/Shutterstock: front cover
b, 4t. Chris Dorney/Shutterstock: front cover t. Mary Evans PL: back cover,
25. © 2014 Hamish Fenton: 5t. Fine Art Images/HIP/Topfoto: 11. Granger
NYC/Alamy: 2c, 27b, 29t. Joan Gravell/Alamy: 10cr. © Peter Gray/Colchester
Museums Services: 21. Dave Head/Shutterstock: 27t. Johnbod/CC Wikimedia:
2ca, 12b. Maxim Khytra/Shutterstock: 10tr. Lowerkase/Dreamstime: 28.
Nature Photos/Shutterstock: 10c. Norfolk Museums Service: 2t, 4b. Paul
Parker/agefotostock/Superstock: 9t. Powered by Light/Alamy: 12t. Simon
Roberts/Rex Shutterstock: 18. © 2016 Roger Massey-Ryan: 19t. Renata
Sedmakova/Shutterstock: 24. Superstock: 14. The Art Archive/Superstock:
1, 13. Vaclav Volrab/Shutterstock: 10cl. Duncan P Walker/istockphoto: 19b.
Stuart Walker/Alamy: 9c, 30. © Rob Watkins/www.robwatkins.co.uk: 29b.
Ian Woolcock/Shutterstock: 10b.

Where did Boudica live?

The Iceni tribe's lands were in modern-day East Anglia, taking in Norfolk and parts of Suffolk and Cambridgeshire. Their capital was near the town of Thetford in Norfolk.

The remains of an important Iceni settlement can be seen at Warham Camp in Norfolk. Historians believe that Iceni people occupied this camp from 200 BCE until just after Boudica's revolt in CE 60/61.

When did Boudica live?

Boudica was born in about CE 25–30. She was probably around 16 years old when the Romans invaded Britain. For people in the ruling families, like Boudica, Roman occupation meant they had to pay more taxes. Some Britons were forced off their land or had to join the Roman army. For many, life carried on much as before.

Why do we still remember Boudica?

Boudica is famous because she united some of the British tribes against the Romans. She led them to victory over the Ninth Legion of the Roman army and her army destroyed three Roman towns. Although her army killed thousands, many people see her as a strong woman who fought for freedom and justice.

BOUDICA'S LIFE STORY

We remember Boudica for the events that took place towards the end of her fairly short life.

1 BOUDICA IS BORN INTO AN IMPORTANT FAMILY IN BRITAIN IN ABOUT CE 25-30.

2

DURING HER CHILDHOOD, BOUDICA LISTENS TO STORIES ABOUT FAMOUS MEMBERS OF HER TRIBE.

3

BOUDICA IS ABOUT 16 YEARS OLD WHEN SHE HEARS NEWS THAT THE ROMAN ARMY HAS LANDED ON THE SOUTH COAST OF BRITAIN.

4

BOUDICA MARRIES KING PRASUTAGUS OF THE ICENI TRIBE.

5 KING PRASUTAGUS HAD MADE AN AGREEMENT WITH THE ROMAN EMPIRE WHICH ALLOWED HIM TO RULE HIS OWN LANDS FOR HIS LIFETIME.

6 AFTER PRASUTAGUS' DEATH, ROMAN SOLDIERS ARRIVE AT BOUDICA'S HOME. THEY WHIP BOUDICA AND TREAT HER DAUGHTERS HARSHLY.

7

Boudica seeks revenge on the Romans. She asks other tribes to join forces with the Iceni against the Romans.

8 Before they set off, a hare runs to the right of a rock, which Boudica sees as a sign that the tribes will win a victory over the Romans.

THE OMEN IS GOOD. IT IS TIME FOR WAR.

9 Boudica's army destroys the Roman town at Colchester. Thousands are killed

10

NOW WE WILL DEFEAT THE ROMAN ARMY!

Thousands more die as Boudica's army destroys Londinium (London) and Verulamium (St Albans).

11

Next, the Roman army chooses a battleground that gives them the advantage. Boudica's huge army is defeated.

12 Boudica escapes but dies soon afterwards. She may have died of an illness or from taking poison.

CELTIC BRITAIN

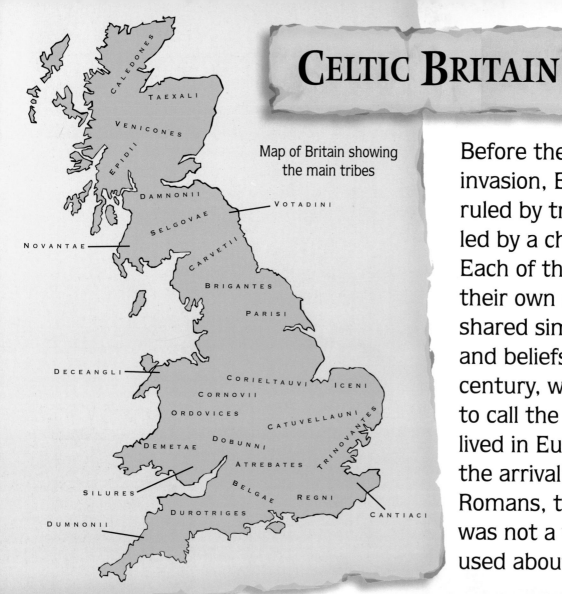

Map of Britain showing the main tribes

Before the Roman invasion, Britain was ruled by tribes, each led by a chief or a king. Each of these tribes had their own customs but shared similar lifestyles and beliefs. In the 16th century, writers started to call the people who lived in Europe before the arrival of the Romans, the Celts. It was not a word they used about themselves.

Tribal wars

Tribes that lived close to each other often fought over control of land. It was quite common for raiding parties to steal cattle and valuable goods from other tribes. Sometimes conflicts could continue for years, with some tribes gaining power over other weaker tribes. All of this helped the Romans when they invaded Britain as they were met by several groups of tribal warriors rather than one large army.

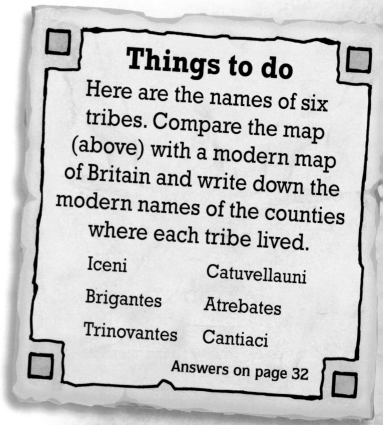

Things to do

Here are the names of six tribes. Compare the map (above) with a modern map of Britain and write down the modern names of the counties where each tribe lived.

Iceni   Catuvellauni

Brigantes   Atrebates

Trinovantes   Cantiaci

Answers on page 32

Roundhouses

We do not have much evidence of life in the Iceni tribe so we use what we know about other Celtic tribes to understand their lives. Boudica probably lived in a large building called a roundhouse. This had a wooden frame, walls made of woven branches covered with dried mud and straw, and a roof of straw or reeds.

Using archaeological evidence, people have reconstructed roundhouses at Castell Henllys in Wales. Earth banks or ditches protected groups of homes.

Warriors went into battle without armour. Some created patterns on their skin using blue dye, as this re-enactor has done.

Farmers... and fighters!

Most people were farmers who lived peacefully on the land they farmed. They tended crops such as wheat and oats and raised their animals. But when their tribal chief called them to battle, they were ready! There are descriptions of them charging into battle with blue patterns on their skin, screaming to terrify the enemy.

FASCINATING FACTS

CELTS BELIEVED THAT WHEN A PERSON DIED THEIR SOUL PASSED TO ANOTHER PERSON. FOR THEM A SOUL NEVER REALLY DIED. THIS GAVE WARRIORS GREAT COURAGE WHEN FIGHTING THEIR ENEMIES.

CELTIC BELIEFS

The Celts worshipped many gods and goddesses and believed that they were everywhere – in their homes and across the countryside.

Worship the natural world

The Celts made offerings to these gods and goddesses in their homes and in special places such as lakes, marshes, moors and forests. Some of these places were used as sites for festivals and other sacred events.

The sky was seen as magical because it was the place out of which came water, light and heat.

Great oak trees seemed to connect the sky to the Earth and were sacred to the Celts.

Celts gathered in woodland clearings to celebrate important events.

Water was sacred. Many Celtic objects have been recovered from Lynn Cerrig Bach on the island of Anglesey, Wales.

Celts worshipped Mother Earth because it produced the food that kept them alive.

The Celts believed that certain hills or mountains had special powers.

Festivals and offerings

Celts celebrated festivals at times of the year that were often linked to the seasons. Festivals were held when seeds were sown in the spring, at harvest time in early autumn, and there were also midwinter and midsummer festivals. It was usual to give offerings to gods and goddesses at these times.

Druids

Celts looked to important people among them, called Druids, for help and guidance in many areas of their lives. They believed that Druids could communicate with the gods and goddesses in various ways, including divination (see below). Druids acted as priests, healers, teachers and judges. The Romans felt threatened by Druids and tried to limit their powers.

Roman writer, Pliny the Elder, who lived in the first century, described a ceremony where a Druid was wearing white robes. This 19th century book illustration shows a Druid at work.

FASCINATING FACTS

DIVINATION IS A WAY OF TRYING TO PREDICT WHAT MIGHT HAPPEN IN THE FUTURE BY INTERPRETING NATURAL EVENTS. CASSIUS DIO, A ROMAN HISTORIAN, TELLS US THAT BOUDICA USED DIVINATION TO SEE WHAT THE OUTCOME OF THE UPRISING WOULD BE BY RELEASING A HARE. WHEN IT RAN TO THE RIGHT SIDE OF A STONE, IT WAS SEEN AS A GOOD SIGN FOR THE BATTLE AHEAD.

CLOTHES AND HAIRSTYLES

Celts took care over their appearance. Some men had moustaches, but not beards, and used lime to make their hair stand up. Like most women, Boudica wore her hair long.

Clothes

Both men and women wore colourful, striped or checked clothes made from wool or linen. The patterns might have looked like tartan fabric still used today. Men dressed in belted tunics and trousers, while women wore long dresses. Both wore woollen cloaks fastened with a brooch to keep them warm.

The Celts dyed wool or linen yarn using plants and berries and then wove the yarn into fabric on looms.

Jewellery

Craftsmen were skilled at using metals to make jewellery. They used bronze, silver and gold, as well as stones, bone and beads to make bracelets, torcs (necklaces), brooches and rings. They decorated them with patterns inspired by nature.

FASCINATING FACTS

IN 1948 A FARMER WAS PLOUGHING A FIELD NEAR SNETTISHAM IN NORFOLK WHEN HE UNEARTHED A GOLD TORC. OVER THE NEXT FEW DECADES, SEVERAL HOARDS OF JEWELLERY AND COINS WERE DISCOVERED IN THE AREA.

The Great Torc found at Snettisham dates from 150–50 BCE and is made from twisted metals.

What did Boudica look like?

As an important person in the tribe, Boudica would have dressed in slightly finer clothes than the rest of the tribe. She also wore beautiful jewellery, including a huge torc around her neck to show her royal status. Cassius Dio (see page 25) wrote this description of Boudica:

A 19th century illustrator imagined that Boudica looked like this.

"Boudica was very tall. She looked terrifying with a fierce glint in her eye. Her voice was harsh. A great mass of bright yellowish-red hair hung down to her hips. Around her neck she had a huge torc of gold. She wore a dress of many colours with a thick cloak over it pinned together with a brooch."

Things to do

Use books or the Internet to find instructions for how to make a simple frame loom. Choose some bright wool and weave a square of fabric.

THE ROMANS ARRIVE

In 54 BCE and 55 BCE, Roman General Julius Caesar led two expeditions to Britain but did not conquer it. The Romans turned their attention to Britain again a hundred years later.

Emperor Claudius

In CE 43, some of the Roman army set sail for Britain under the orders of Emperor Claudius. Claudius needed a military victory over Britain to give Roman citizens a reason to like and respect him. By conquering Britain he would achieve something that even Julius Caesar had failed to do. Claudius also wanted to get access to Britain's silver, gold and tin mines.

FASCINATING FACTS

CLAUDIUS WAS UNLUCKY IN LOVE. HIS FIRST WEDDING WAS CALLED OFF AT THE LAST MINUTE. HIS SECOND 'BRIDE TO BE' DIED ON THEIR WEDDING DAY. HE WAS MARRIED FOUR TIMES IN ALL AND HIS LAST WIFE KILLED HIM BY GIVING HIM POISONOUS MUSHROOMS!

A bronze head of Emperor Claudius made in the 1st century. It once formed part of a statue of Claudius outside the Temple of Claudius in Colchester, Essex.

The Roman invasion

When the Romans invaded Britain with around 40,000 men, they met fierce resistance from the Catuvellauni (see map, page 8). By making peace agreements with some tribes and conquering others, the Romans soon controlled much of southern Britain. They named their new lands 'Britannia'.

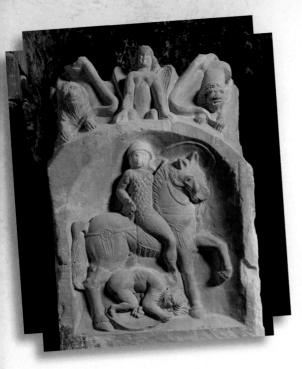

The carvings on the tombstone of Longinus, a Roman soldier who took part in the invasion of Britain, show him riding over the top of a defeated tribesman.

Victory procession

Emperor Claudius travelled from Italy to Britain in order to lead his army into Camulodunum, now called Colchester. His victory procession included elephants and no one had seen anything like it before. Several British chiefs knelt before Claudius to offer their surrender. When Claudius returned to Rome, people celebrated his victory again. Claudius was so thrilled he named his son Britannicus.

An Arch of Claudius was built in Rome to commemorate the conquest of Britain, as shown on this gold coin dating from that time.

Things to do

Imagine what it was like for someone like Boudica to hear about a great army from a far away place landing in her country. Write a diary entry about Boudica's feelings.

Peace with Rome

The Iceni made a peace agreement with the Romans. In return for showing loyalty to the Roman Empire, they were left to rule themselves. Boudica's husband, King Prasutagus, was probably made a citizen of the Roman Empire.

15

THE DEATH OF PRASUTAGUS

When Emperor Claudius died in CE 54 his stepson, Nero, became the new emperor. In CE 58 Emperor Nero sent the army general, Suetonius Paulinus, to be the new governor of Britain. Relationships between the Romans and the British tribes were about to change.

> It is the year 59. King Prasutagus of the Iceni has just died. His will left instructions for his kingdom to be shared between Emperor Nero and his daughters. He hoped this arrangement would be accepted by Nero, and that Nero would allow half the Iceni lands to be ruled by Prasutagus' daughters.

Boudica watched as King Prasutagus' body was placed on the cold earth. His sword, belt and torc were laid beside him, along with a bronze cup and other items he would need in the afterlife. As the soil piled over his body Boudica turned away, tears streaming down her face. Her husband, Prasutagus, had gone from her world.

News of the death of King Prasutagus soon reached the ears of important Romans in Britain, including Decianus Catus. He was the imperial procurator, responsible for collecting taxes, and he was a young man intent on making a name for himself.

'She said what?' bellowed Decianus at the centurion standing to attention in the centre of the room.

'Boudica said that Prasutagus has left half of everything he owned to Emperor Nero and half to his two daughters.'

'That woman has some cheek. If she thinks the Roman Empire will keep an agreement we had with her husband then she is in for a shock. Nero does not bargain with a woman, even if she is the leader of her tribe,' said Decianus Catus.

Boudica had hoped that Emperor Nero and his representatives in Britain would allow her daughters to inherit half of their father's lands. However, this was not to be. Decianus Catus ordered his men to seize Iceni land and valuables, claiming them for the Roman Empire.

Re-enactors dressed as Roman soldiers.

The first the Iceni knew of the approaching trouble was when a group of women appeared on the hillside, shouting and pointing to the south. As soon as Boudica caught sight of the Roman soldiers marching across the landscape, she sensed trouble.

Women grabbed hold of their children and scattered as the soldiers marched into the village. They had not come to make deals but to make an example of Boudica.

She cursed them as they entered her royal home. Clinging to her daughters she called on the gods to hurl down fire on the Romans, but her pleas went unanswered. Boudica was tied to a post.

The leather whip bit deep into her flesh. It felt as if she had been stung by a swarm of bees. She watched helplessly as her daughters were passed from one soldier to another to be mocked, to be teased, to be taught a lesson.

Iceni men, stripped of their weapons, stripped of their courage, watched on as their queen and their tribe was humiliated. But a fire began to burn in the hearts and minds of the Iceni that day. It would soon turn into a blaze that would ignite a fire of rebellion across the east of England.

In their dealings with the Iceni and the Trinovantes the Romans were harsh, taking over land, raising taxes and stealing treasures. But in the year 60 or 61, the Iceni and Trinovantes tribes would have their revenge.

WARRIOR QUEEN

Boudica is often shown riding on a chariot with weapons in her hands. She has became a symbol for any woman who fights for freedom.

The making of a warrior

After Roman soldiers flogged Boudica and treated her daughters cruelly, Boudica began to plan her revenge. She was prepared to wage war against the Romans in Britain until she was dead, or the Romans had been driven from the shores of Britain by the native tribes.

Warrior queen?

Roman historians tell us that she led the rebellion but we do not know whether she had the fighting skills needed to be a warrior queen. The historians describe how she gave a great speech to her warriors from her chariot. She rode up and down the lines of men with her daughters standing beside her. She may not have actually fought in the final battle (see page 23) but may have watched from a safe distance.

Actress Alex Kingston played Boudica in the film *Boudica*, released in 2003.

Joining forces

Boudica knew that if she wanted to defeat the Roman army then she needed more warriors – thousands more! She turned to the Trinovantes tribe who lived in what is now Essex.

The Temple of Claudius in Camulodunum (now Colchester) was a hated symbol of Roman power over the Trinovantes. This illustration was produced with the help of archaeologists.

The Trinovantes had their own reasons to hate the Roman occupiers. First the Romans had built an army fort on top of their capital at Camulodunum (now called Colchester). A few years later they turned the fort into a town for retired soldiers and their families. In addition, the Trinovantes were forced to pay high taxes to pay for the building of a temple to Emperor Claudius.

HISTORY LINKS

During the reign of Elizabeth I (1558–1603), writers compared their queen to Boudica. With England threatened by the Spanish Armada in 1588, Elizabeth I gave a powerful speech to her troops, gathered on the docks at Tilbury, just as Boudica did as leader of her army.

Boudica's army advanced towards Colchester, its first target. The year was 60 or 61.

Retirement town

Because Colchester was an undefended *colonia*, a settlement for retired Roman soldiers and their families, it had no defensive walls or earth banks to keep out Boudica's army.

Boudica's timing was perfect. The Roman governor of Britain, Seutonius Paulinus, had taken some of his army to Anglesey, off the coast of Wales. Although soldiers of the Ninth Legion of the Roman army set off from Lincoln to help defend Colchester, Boudica's army ambushed them, killing many. As Boudica's forces drew closer, the citizens of Colchester must have been terrified.

FASCINATING FACTS

IN SEPTEMBER 2014, ARCHAEOLOGISTS DISCOVERED ROMAN JEWELLERY AND COINS THAT HAD BEEN BURIED IN THE FLOOR OF A COLCHESTER HOUSE IN THE YEAR 60 OR 61. THEY THINK THAT A ROMAN COUPLE MUST HAVE BURIED THEIR VALUABLES TO HIDE THEM FROM BOUDICA'S APPROACHING ARMY. THEIR HOME WAS DESTROYED BY FIRE. DID THE FAMILY ESCAPE? THEY NEVER CAME BACK FOR THEIR VALUABLES.

Some of the Roman objects discovered in 2014 in Colchester. From top left: a gold bracelet, coins, gold rings and gold earrings.

Colchester is destroyed

Boudica's army swept into the town with ease. They showed no mercy, killing thousands and setting fire to buildings in the town. Hundreds of people ran inside the Temple of Claudius and barricaded themselves inside, hoping that help would arrive. After two days, Boudica's followers set the temple on fire with the people still trapped inside. Colchester was reduced to ruins.

An artist's impression of the Temple of Claudius in ruins.

News reaches Rome

The news of Boudica's attack on Colchester travelled fast. It wasn't long before Emperor Nero, back in Rome, heard of Boudica's revolt. He was horrified. How could the Ninth Legion have been defeated and the settlements destroyed? He considered pulling the army out of Britain altogether.

Leaving Colchester behind them, Boudica's army set off for London. Although Suetonius Paulinus reached London before Boudica's army, he realised he could not defend the town. Instead he advised people to leave and left London to its fate.

The map shows the progress of Boudica's army, destroying three Roman towns before meeting the Roman army somewhere in the Midlands.

The destruction continues

When Boudica and her army arrived in London they found it deserted and undefended. As they had in Colchester, they set fire to buildings and killed anyone who had stayed behind. In particular they focused their hatred on noble Roman women, killing them in horrible ways.

The town of Verulamium (St Albans) suffered the same fate. Roman writer Tacitus (see page 24) wrote that Boudica's forces took no prisoners. "They could not wait to cut throats, hang, burn and crucify..." The town was burnt to the ground, like London and Colchester.

The Battle of Watling Street

Boudica's army moved on, travelling along Watling Street. This time the Roman army was waiting for them. Suetonius Paulinus, the Roman commander, chose the site of the battle. He placed his army in a steep-sided valley with a forest behind it for protection. Boudica's warriors had to launch their attack over open ground.

A re-enactment of the Battle of Watling Street. People dressed as Boudica's warriors struggle against a Roman shield wall.

By this time Boudica's army had grown in size to possibly 230,000 people, far more than the Roman forces of about 10,000. Despite this, the Romans won. Their army was well trained, had better weapons and Suetonius Paulinus was very experienced.

When Boudica's army tried to retreat, they were delayed by their own wagons, placed at the end of the valley for their supporters to stand on. The Romans killed thousands of Iceni and other warriors, as well as women and children. Boudica escaped but died soon afterwards from an illness or by taking poison.

My own research

Before he was appointed as governor of Britain, Seutonius Paulinus had fought in several places across the Roman Empire. He was the very first Roman to cross the Atlas Mountains. Use a map to find out where they are.

Answer on page 32

HOW DO WE KNOW?

The Iceni did not write things down, so the only written records we have about Boudica come from two Roman writers, Tacitus and Cassius Dio.

Tacitus

Tacitus was a small boy living in Italy when Boudica launched her rebellion. But his wife's father, Julius Agricola, was a soldier in the army that fought Boudica at the Battle of Watling Street. This meant that Tacitus was able to find out lots of information from Julius Agricola, a living witness, which he later wrote down in Latin.

His account of the events in 60 or 61 includes a description of events just prior to the Battle of Watling Street:

"Boudica drove around all the tribes in a chariot with her daughters in front of her. 'We British are used to women commanders in war,' she cried. 'I am descended from mighty men! But I am not fighting for my kingdom and wealth now. I am fighting as an ordinary person for my lost freedom, my bruised body, and my outraged daughters.'"

This 19th century statue of Tacitus (56–117) stands outside the Parliament building in Vienna, Austria.

Cassius Dio

The Roman writer, Cassius Dio, wrote a long history of the Romans in his language, Greek. He was born almost a hundred years after Boudica had died, but he may have read documents about Boudica that have since disappeared. In the case of Boudica's death, Cassius Dio tells a slightly longer version of Boudica's last hours than Tacitus, who wrote, "Boudica killed herself with poison."

An 18th century portrait of Cassius Dio (150–235).

"Many Britons were cut down in the battle and before the wagons and the woods. Many too were taken alive. Some, however, escaped and made preparations to fight again, but when in the meantime Boudica fell ill and died the Britons mourned her deeply and gave her a lavish funeral, and then they disbanded in the belief that now they really were defeated."

What do you think?

Which of these Roman writers do you think is more reliable? Give your reasons.

FASCINATING FACTS

ARCHAEOLOGISTS HAVE FOUND LAYERS OF BURNT BUILDING MATERIALS UNDER EACH OF THE FORMER ROMAN SETTLEMENTS AT COLCHESTER, ST ALBANS AND LONDON. ARCHAEOLOGISTS DATE THE BURNT LAYERS TO 60 OR 61, WHICH BACKS UP THE ACCOUNTS OF BOTH TACITUS AND CASSIUS DIO.

WHAT HAPPENED NEXT?

After Boudica's uprising failed, the Romans rebuilt the towns of Colchester, London and St Albans.

Roman Britain

By the end of the first century, the Romans controlled most of southern Britain, including Wales. Later they added parts of Scotland to their empire. Some of the people who had once belonged to tribes started to change to a Roman way of life. They moved to towns, visited the public baths, watched plays and chariot races and spoke Latin. In other places, people continued to follow their own way of life or just adopted a few Roman customs.

The Roman baths at Bath were built over the top of a hot spring that was sacred to the tribe who lived there when the Romans arrived.

Under attack

Britain remained part of the Roman Empire for almost four hundred years. But in the early 5th century, Rome itself was under almost constant attack from tribes outside the Empire. More troops were needed to defend Rome and other parts of the Empire, so the Roman army was withdrawn from Britain.

The Saxons arrive

Even before the Roman army had left, tribes from what is now Germany (Saxons) and then Denmark (Angles) began to raid towns and villages along the east coast of England. Some of them settled alongside the people of Britain, bringing their language and way of life to Britain.

This 12th century illustration shows Angles and Saxons crossing the sea to Britain.

BOUDICA LIVES ON

Boudica died almost two thousand years ago yet we still remember her today. Through history, her story has been kept alive, often because other women leaders are linked with Boudica.

Boudica and Queen Elizabeth I

During the reign of Elizabeth I, writers compared their queen to Queen Boudica. Elizabeth I even claimed she was descended from the same family as Boudica. They both had long, rusty brown hair and gave a powerful speech to their army just before an important battle (see pages 18–19). They were both strong, inspiring women in a world where there were very few female leaders.

A strong queen

Next to the River Thames and the Houses of Parliament stands a statue of Boudica and her daughters riding a war chariot. It was commissioned by Prince Albert, Queen Victoria's husband, to celebrate her long reign (1837–1901). As a strong ruler who fought for Britain's freedom, it seemed a good idea to compare Boudica to Queen Victoria.

Boudica's statue, sculpted by Thomas Thornycroft, was placed next to the River Thames in 1902.

A banner with Boudica's name on it was carried by women campaigning for the vote in the early part of the 20th century.

Rights for women

From the mid 19th century until 1928, women campaigned to be able to vote in elections. Boudica became one of their heroines, a strong woman who stood up for herself and fought for what was right. Her name appeared on one of the fabric banners used in processions through the streets of London and pictures of her appeared on posters, badges and leaflets promoting the campaign.

A protective parent

There is a statue of Boudica and her daughters in Cardiff City Hall in Wales. The sculptor, J Havard Thomas, shows Boudica not as a warrior but as a protective, loving mother. We do not know what became of Boudica's daughters after her death.

The statue of Boudica and her daughters in Cardiff City Hall was installed in 1916.

Things to do

Now you have read this book, which of these words would you use to describe Boudica? Give reasons for your answers.

bossy wild brave daring
fiery ruthless foolish cruel
independent heroic

BUDDUG
BOADICEA

DIED AD 61

J HAVARD THOMAS
SCULPTOR

29

TIMELINE

55/54 BCE
JULIUS CAESAR LEADS TWO
EXPEDITIONS TO BRITAIN BUT SOON
RETURNS TO GAUL (MODERN FRANCE)

60 BCE

50 BCE

40 BCE

44 BCE
JULIUS CAESAR,
RULER OF ROME,
IS MURDERED

30 BCE

27 BCE
AUGUSTUS
BECOMES THE
FIRST EMPEROR

20 BCE

10 BCE

0

c.4 BCE
BIRTH OF
JESUS
CHRIST

49
COLCHESTER BECOMES
A COLONIA, HOME
TO RETIRED ROMAN
SOLDIERS

47
ICENI TRIBE REVOLT
AGAINST A ROMAN
ORDER TO GIVE UP
THEIR WEAPONS BUT THE
REVOLT IS PUT DOWN

41
CLAUDIUS BECOMES
EMPEROR

20

**c. CE
25–30**
BOUDICA IS
BORN

51
CARATACUS,
KING OF THE
CATUVELLAUNI
TRIBE, IS
CAPTURED BY
THE ROMANS
AND TAKEN
TO ROME

40

54
NERO BECOMES
EMPEROR

43
ROMAN ARMY
INVADES SOUTHERN
BRITAIN

58
SUETONIUS
PAULINUS
BECOMES
GOVERNOR
OF BRITAIN

60

c.60/61
SUETONIUS
PAULINUS
TAKES TROOPS
TO ANGLESEY
(KNOWN AS
MONA) IN WALES
TO SUBDUE
DRUIDS

c.60/61
KING PRASUTAGUS OF THE ICENI TRIBE DIES

❋

BOUDICA LEADS A REVOLT AGAINST THE ROMAN
OCCUPIERS

❋

BOUDICA'S ARMY ATTACKS COLCHESTER,
LONDON AND ST ALBANS

❋

BOUDICA'S ARMY IS DEFEATED AT THE BATTLE
OF WATLING STREET

c.77
THE ROMANS
FINALLY
CONQUER
WALES

80

79
MOUNT VESUVIUS
ERUPTS AND
DESTROYS POMPEII
AND HERCULANEUM

100

122
EMPEROR HADRIAN ORDERS
THAT A WALL BE BUILT
ACROSS NORTHERN BRITAIN

120

c.142
ROMANS BUILD THE
ANTONINE WALL IN
SCOTLAND

140

GLOSSARY

Afterlife a life that some people believe exists after death

Centurion an officer in the Roman army who commanded about 80 soldiers

Customs the usual or accepted way of behaving or doing something in a place or within a group of people

Governor in Roman Britain, the person in charge of Britain

Hoard an ancient store of coins and valuable items

Imperial procurator an important Roman official, responsible for the Roman Empire's finances

Justice fair treatment or behaviour

Legion a large group of soldiers (between 4,000–6,000) within the Roman army

Lime a white substance obtained from limestone

Noble in Roman society, someone who was born into a family at the top of society

Omen an event that is taken as a sign that something is about to happen

Roman citizen someone in Roman society who had privileges that were not offered to other non-citizens, such as holding an important job

Roman Empire ruled from its centre of power in Rome, modern Italy, the Roman Empire stretched across Europe, North Africa and parts of Asia

Sacred connected with religion

Spanish Armada a fleet of Spanish warships sent to attack England in 1588

Tribe a group of people, often related to each other, who live together and share a similar way of life, beliefs and language

Will a person's wishes for what will happen to their possessions after their death

THE GREAT QUEEN BOUDICA QUIZ

1. Roughly how old was Boudica when the Romans invaded Britain?

2. Which tribe did Boudica belong to?

3. What name did the Romans give to Britain?

4. Which writer gave us a description of Boudica's appearance?

5. Who was the Roman emperor when Boudica's army attacked the Roman army?

6. What is a torc?

7. Which Tudor queen compared herself to Boudica?

8. Who did Boudica marry?

9. What are the names of the places Boudica's army attacked?

10. Who led the Roman army to defeat Boudica's army?

11. Where did the Saxons and Angles come from?

12. Where can you see the famous statue of Boudica standing on her chariot?

NOW WE WILL DEFEAT THE ROMAN ARMY!

Answers on page 32

31

INDEX

Angles 27
archaeologists 9, 19, 20, 25
Battle of Watling Street 7, 18, 22–24
beliefs, Celtic 8, 9, 10–11, 16, 26
Boudica
 appearance 12, 13
 daughters 4, 6, 16–18, 24, 28, 29
 death 7, 23, 25
 early life 5, 6
 leads the uprising 4–5, 18–23
 marriage 4, 6
 statues of 4, 28–29
Caesar, Julius 14
Camulodunum 5, 7, 15, 19–22, 25, 26
Cassius Dio 4, 11, 13, 18, 24–25
Catuvellauni 8, 15
chariots, war 18, 24, 28
clothes, Celtic 12–13
Colchester 5, 7, 14, 15, 19–22, 25, 26

Decianus Catus 16
divination 7, 11
Druids 11
Emperor Claudius 14–16, 19
Emperor Hadrian 27
Emperor Nero 16, 21
farming 9, 11
festivals 10, 11
gods/goddesses 10–11, 17
Hadrian's Wall 27
hairstyles 12–13
Iceni 4–9, 15, 16–24
jewellery 12, 13, 20
King Prasutagus 4, 6, 15, 16
Lincoln 20, 22
London/Londinium 5, 7, 22, 25, 26
Ninth Legion 5, 7, 20, 21
Queen Elizabeth I 19, 28
Queen Victoria 28
Roman army 4–7, 14–24, 27

Roman baths, Bath 26
Roman Empire 6, 15, 16, 23, 26–27
Roman invasion 4–6, 8, 14–15
roundhouses 9
St Albans 5, 7, 22, 25, 26
Saxons 27
Seutonius Paulinus 16, 20, 22–23
Spanish Armada 19
suffragettes/suffragists 29
Tacitus 4, 18, 22, 24–25
taxes 5, 16, 17, 19
Temple of Claudius 14, 19, 21
torcs 12, 13, 16
tribes, British 4–9, 13, 15–24, 26
Trinovantes 8, 17, 19–23
Verulamium 5, 7, 22, 25, 26
warriors, British 8–9, 17–23
weaving 12–13

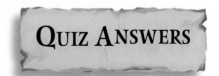

QUIZ ANSWERS

Things to do, page 8 : Iceni = Norfolk and parts of Suffolk and Cambridgeshire;
Catuvellauni = Hertfordshire, Bedfordshire and Cambridgeshire;
Brigantes = most of Yorkshire, Cleveland, Durham and Lancashire;
Atrebates = West Sussex, Hampshire and Berkshire;
Trinovantes = Essex and part of Suffolk; **Cantiaci** = Kent.

My own research, page 23:
the Atlas Mountains are in north-west Africa (Morocco, Algeria and Tunisia).

The Great Queen Boudica Quiz, page 31
1. 16 years old **2.** Iceni **3.** Britannia **4.** Cassius Dio **5.** Emperor Nero **6.** A heavy piece of jewellery worn round the neck
7. Queen Elizabeth I **8.** King Prasutagus **9.** Colchester, London, St Albans **10.** Suetonius Paulinus
11. Germany and Denmark **12.** London, near the Houses of Parliament